Success Comes in Cans

How To Grow a Miracle In 21 Days

c.w. Pickett

乜

Mushin Press

Table of Contents

HAPPINESS MUST HAPPEN.
THE SAME HOLDS TRUE FOR SUCCESS.
YOU HAVE TO LET IT HAPPEN...
BY NOT CARING ABOUT IT.

Viktor Frankle

This Book is Dedicated to My Father.
A Most Exceptional Man.

Forethoughts

This book can change your life.

Are you feeling stuck and cannot seem to find a way out of the rut? Do you have plans but they just are not happening fast enough? Try these three simple principles: Observe, Reframe, and Plan.

For the next three weeks, make a commitment to give your full attention to what you want to accomplish. Stick with it for 21 days, and you will surprise yourself when you say, "It's a miracle!"

Let me show you how.

In his later years, my dad took to doing needle point. As a farmer and a carpenter, he was always busy with his hands. Even in retirement, never a man to sit, he made miniature furniture for doll houses and made needle points with quotes and words of wisdom.

One has hung in my kitchen for years. It says:

> *Success comes in cans.*
> *Failure comes in can'ts.*

Growing a miracle takes a success mindset. You must ditch the negative thoughts. "Easier said than done," is the most common comment from people when talking about ridding negative thoughts. Yes, I agree one hundred percent. Switching your mind from negative thoughts to successful thoughts takes a lot of practice and concentration. A very tiring project!

The point of this book is to make the progress to success easier. Misplaced thinking leads us to believe changing our thoughts alone will change our life. New science confirms that the stress and trauma from growing up and living in this world not only shapes our thoughts, but also our nervous and endocrine systems. How do you change what childhood has ingrained in you?

Those crazy thoughts, the racing mind, the burning brain - your nervous system is firing out of control. The psychological factors that accompany stress and trauma is not "all in your head."

Our response to life is not something we can just "think" away. But at the same time, there is life to live, problems to solve, major stressors to deal with. How do you find the time to work on your goals with all that going on?

As you will see further in this book, all it takes is fifteen minutes a day. For three weeks. This 21-day miracle is simple to implement. Have a goal but feel stuck? Take the 21-day miracle challenge by observing your thoughts and behaviors as to why you feel stuck, reframing those thoughts and behaviors, and making a plan to propel you forward.

At the end of the 21 days, you will say, "I did it. I grew a miracle!"

One miracle builds on another. This is a handy technique for solving any problem that arises.

Without further ado – let me show you how to grow a miracle in 21 days.

Chapter 1

FROM STUCK TO SUCCESS IN 21 DAYS

Are you stuck in a rut? You have great ambitions but cannot get past the "logistics" of why you are stuck in your dreams or how to make them a reality.

If you are reading this, you have probably tried multiple times to get over this sensation of stuckedness, but so far, you have not figured out how to get out of the way of yourself.

Do not feel bad. Stuckedness seems to be a societal anomaly these days. People are caught in the rat race of 9 to 5 and cannot break away. They want to pursue their dreams, but the reality of their regular day takes up too much time and energy.

How will you ever break out of the doldrums?

My book has arrived to answer this question. The idea came from Ed Rush's book, *The 21 Day Miracle: How To Change Anything in 3 Short Weeks*. He writes about how as a fighter pilot he learned to fly in 21 days. How the military did nothing but drill, drill, drill until the young recruit who was afraid of his shadow became a solo pilot of the most expensive planes in the world! How does this work?

I am here to tell you. Three weeks, three steps. Depending on how seriously you take this "miracle making business" will depend on the success of your "success." This is a purely personal journey. You get out of it what you put into it.

Ed Rush talks about how in the first week he thought about kicking the wall and breaking his toe so he could go home. He thought about this a few times over the first week. But he got over it, and realized he really did like the vigorous training. This will also happen to you. There will be a point in the first week where you want to give up. "This is really stupid," you tell yourself. But you made a commitment for 21 days. Now, make up your mind to stick with it. What's 21 days out of a lifetime? Good things might come out of this after all.

If the military can train a wet-behind-the-ears recruit in 21 days to become a fighter pilot, why can't you make your dreams a reality? Maybe not learn to fly a plane (you could if you so desired). What occupies your mind, keeps you awake at night?

Start with a small task to test the waters to convince yourself that believing is not difficult. Believing is what this boils down to. Believing that you can, and will, accomplish what you set out to do.

Little steps. Here is an example of how you can apply the 21-day plan:

Observe, Reframe, Plan.

Please do not be disgusted by my example. A daunting task for most of us is to control the clutter in our house. Often just a small routine can ease the stress of getting your act together. Say you are lax on cleaning out the cat box. This bothers you and everyone around you, but you hate the job and you put it off as long as you can.

The first week **observe** your actions. How many times do you change the litter in that week? How do you feel while you are changing it? What excuses do you give yourself when it comes time to do the deed? Observe. Be a witness to your thoughts and actions. No judgements, no difference in your routine. Just observe.

The next week, **reframe**. The first week, you learned why you hate changing the litter box, the second week, reframe those thoughts. You observed your routine and realized that changing it more often would make a big difference in the way your house smells. This week, you work on reframing those impressions and find cues to get the job done in a timely manner.

The third week, make a **plan**. How often will you change the litter box? How can you make your job easier so it is not so disgusting?

And then **celebrate**. Give yourself kudos for taking the time to make this one job so much easier. Congratulate yourself through the weeks ahead. "I'm so glad I figured this out!"

Changing the cat box also takes on a figurative form. People often move their "poop" from one place to the next, covering it up as best they can. Rather than tackle the problem head on, we have a tendency to "hide and deny" and repeat the same useless routines over and over again. And then wonder why we are stuck.

This simplistic example can be applied to whatever you feel you need to fix about yourself. Want to lose a few pounds? Feel the need to exercise more? How about finding a job you enjoy, or starting a business? Stuck in how to accomplish your dreams?

I have used this method many times. The first attempt was looking at my mindset for finances. Conditioning through our lifetime tells us how to think about money. If we have a scarcity mindset, we live in scarcity. Miracles of miracles, once I discovered why I felt about money the way I did, my financial situation improved.

For the first week, pay close attention to your thinking patterns 24/7. Good thing it is only for 7 days, right? Observing your thoughts and feelings is exhausting. You might go places in your memories you have been avoiding. You will feel uncomfortable. This process is necessary, as hard as it is. Searching for a truth about yourself is not an easy journey. This is why the desire to give up that first week is so strong. No way do you want to go down the path your thoughts are taking you.

But do you want to be shackled by your thoughts of fear and doubt, or do you want to break free of what is holding you back? Do you want to explore different ways to live? This could mean changing your spending habits, or your eating habits. Little steps pertinent to your life.

Once you gain confidence in this system after the first 21 days, you will realize there are other parts of your life open to miracles.

This is important to remember when doubts creep in. Have you ever said to your child, "When did you get so tall?" Changes in your life are just as gradual. One day you notice a difference; those changes you made three weeks ago are showing up.

A Miracle would not be a Miracle if it could be explained.

Chapter 2

WHY I AM WRITING THIS BOOK

Reading Ed Rush's book was not the first time I witnessed this 21-day miracle in action. It happened in our karate class, but at the time, I did not know why the students made such great progress so quickly. I assumed it was the expertise of the instructor. And indeed. Trained in the martial arts since age six, his natural path was to join the military as an adult. There, as part of his Special Forces training, he also learned what the military teaches to all new recruits:

How to become a soldier in 21 days.

This works in your daily life, in the dojo (karate training hall), and obviously works for the military. We have the most excellent troops in the world, highly trained to meet any threat to Americans, foreign or domestic.

Within six weeks, our students were ready to progress to the next rank. Their techniques were crisp and clean, and they knew the material. How did this happen?

Teach. Demonstrate. Do. Just like they train fighter pilots.

Do you want to live a life that is true to yourself and not what others think you "should" be doing? Are you hung up in society and family expectations and have lost sight of what you want out of life?

The best way to get out of these doldrums is to set small goals. The big question people carry in their head is, "What is my purpose in life?" For now, let us focus on those small steps that lead to introspection. Introspection leads to your purpose.

Observe your thoughts and actions, question why you do what you do, then start digging for the answer. Watch for a thinking pattern, a misbelief, an annoying habit.

Jim Collins writes of the hedgehog concept in his book _Good to Great_. All great companies drill down the _"one thing"_ that drives their business. After studying multiple successful businesses, he found there are variations to the theme, but one thing rules their profits. For example, Walmart has many items in their stores, but their "one thing" is to keep prices low.

> ### What drives me?
>
> What am I better at than anyone else?
> What am I most passionate about?
> What drives my economic engine?

Once you put these three answers together, you find the skill and talent that is uniquely yours. The first step in the first week is to figure out which miracle you want to see first.

You chuckle, smirk into your hand. A miracle. Right. I get it. It sounds crazy, doesn't it? I approached Ed Rush's idea tentatively, just like you are, but was ready for change because nothing was moving. Stuck. What did it cost to try?

Yes, I have experienced the meaning of stuckedness. You just cannot get over the hump of what is holding you back. You have tried it all. You listened to all the advice on YouTube, to the self-help gurus like Wayne Dyer and Mel Robbins, but all that good advice just does not seem to apply to you.

There are many reasons why I feel this way, as I am sure you can attest to for yourself. Working out the logistics often leads to seemingly unsurmountable obstacles. Perhaps you are not willing to upset the apple cart, or uproot your family, or there is a fear holding you back.

Meet the brutal reality of your situation.

My first trek was straightening out my finances. Like for many of us post-COVID, money is tight, to say the least. For me, it was time to change my standard option of doing nothing.

Week one, I observed my spending habits and my thoughts on the subject, and delved into my past, hearing those voices that trained me in my limiting beliefs. "When our ship comes in," was one of my mom's favorite phrases. Naturally, living in mountain country, the ship never came in. She grew up during the Depression of the 1930s, and not having money then affected her outlook for the rest of her life…and guess what, she passed it down to me.

She taught me to be thrifty and how to make what I need instead of buying it. These skills have come in handy several times in my life. But so did the limiting beliefs (not so handy).

She also taught me that money was scarce, and it was not your friend. Those realizations alerted me to how screwed up that thinking was. "Not your friend," does not stick around, so why would you accumulate wealth? It is not as we are taught, that money is the source of all evil, which is a misquote to start with. Money is cold, hard cash. It represents a piece of gold or silver. Nothing else. There is nothing "evil" about money, it is not wrong to be rich.

Whew, that was a tough week. No wonder I wanted to quit halfway through. But I am not a quitter, so I persevered. Did this miracle making really work? Had to see it to the end to find out!

The second week, I reframed my thinking and reorganized my spending habits. Week one showed where I was wasting money and where to eliminate unnecessary expenses. Week two gave me a chance to correct that. Gave myself pats on the back for making it this far.

Week three was to make a plan. How will I go forward with my new-found knowledge? There was still work to be done from week two, it takes a while to eliminate those unnecessary expenses and whittle down those monthly payments. But by now, the train wreck my finances had become was starting to get back on track, and I was beginning to breathe easier.

Was that a miracle or what? To go from nerve-wracking indecision and uncertainty to a plan and confidence it will work – all in three short weeks. Notice, my objective was not any great goal.

I just wanted to have peace of mind and to put my finances in order. That is exactly what I accomplished. a miracle.

Stuck is no longer in your vocabulary.
Now you know the meaning of success.

Chapter 3

DO WHAT YOU LOVE AND THE MONEY WILL FOLLOW

Do you believe that? If you do, wealth will follow you. Who would not want to make countless amounts of money for doing what they love?

What do you love to do? What interests you more than anything? What do you spend your time dreaming about? "If only I had a million dollars, I could…" Wouldn't that be great?

But riches that come about with hard work, tears, and blood, are much more appreciated than if a great aunt handed you six million dollars. Few of us have rich aunts lying around, so the only way we will acquire wealth is by growing our money the right way.

But first, you must make money. Hate your job? Struggling from paycheck to paycheck? Living off credit cards at the end of the month? Gotta feed those kids! You know it is inflation when your paycheck does not meet your means, and you are living within your means.

Your first journey into the miracle world may not be finances. Maybe you want to get in shape.

Brick by Brick. Make it Stick.

As self-improvement guru Mel Robbins says: Brick by Brick. Make it Stick. A house is not built overnight. Rome was not built overnight. Change is gradual. You rarely see it until you have an ah-ha moment.

There are a lot of rich-quick schemes out there. The internet is full of them. These schemes are like gym memberships. You pay big dollars up front, eager to learn this new trade, but after a few weeks, you find this is not as interesting or as easy as the producers made it sound.

Following this 21-day miracle plan, though, as you discover traits you did not know you had, one thing is guaranteed. The results will spur you on to bigger successes.

THE FOX KNOWS MANY THINGS,

BUT THE HEDGEHOG KNOWS ONLY ONE "BIG" THING.

The Hedgehog Concept

I mentioned the hedgehog concept in the earlier chapter, now we will expound on that and explore what being a hedgehog really means. A hedgehog has spines, but unlike a porcupine, they are not poisonous, and they do not shoot out at you. They live in New Zealand, Europe, Asia, and Africa, and considering they eat one-third of their weight every day, you could say their "passion" is foraging for food.

What is your "one big thing?" Let us break it down.

1. Does this activity bring me great joy?
2. Do I look forward to the work necessary to pursue this activity?
3. Do I believe in what I am doing?

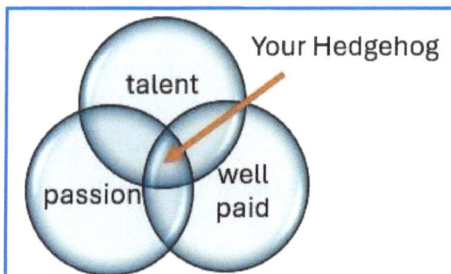

Talent: I was born to do this.

Passion: I love to do this.

Well paid: Do what you love and the money will follow.

The hedgehog concept is a simple, crystalline concept that appears at the intersection of these three qualities.

Stick to what you understand, and let ability, not ego, determine your path.

More questions to ask:

What are my abilities?
What am I best at?
What am I worst at?

> *A tiger communicates only with tigers.*
> *A dog communicates only with dogs.*
> *What is your job?*
> a Buddhist koan

What is your job? What is your passion? What unique gift can you give to the world?

Focus on what you can do better than anyone else.

If you want to improve your work situation, my advice is this:

Week one: Observe your thoughts, your work habits. No judgement, no worries, just observe. Look for the underlying reasons you feel the way you do.

Week two: Reframe your thoughts. Can you modify your work habits? Did you discover why you are unhappy with your job? Can you see ways to make it better? Can you look for another job?

Week one and two. Other than journalling, observing, and reflecting, no other action is necessary. Before you can implement a plan, you must know what plan you want to implement. For now, you are just gathering information and coming up with ideas. Through journalling and reflection, you will find answers to the question of "what is your big thing?"

Week three: Make a plan. By now you should have a good idea of why you do feel the way you do. Begin to apply easy steps. By the end of the week, you will have a plan. You will know if it is time to quit your job and move on, start that business, or – nothing. Doing nothing is an option, you know. Perhaps now is not the right time, but you do not stop there.

After 21 days, you will know. You will either continue to pursue this train of thought, or you will find better alternatives. The journey is not over in 21 days. You are just getting started!

Do not forget to Celebrate!! You just witnessed a miracle!

Week four and beyond: The implementation of your plan. You may only be able to devote 15 minutes a day, but now you are motivated and look forward to those 15 minutes. Brick by brick, progress will happen faster than you expect.

Once you discover this trick really does work, you will find other ways to improve your life – all in a matter of 21 days.

Best and worst, one must have an understanding of what you can be and what you cannot be.

Chapter 4

THINK YOUR WAY THIN

At some point in life, the body morphed out of shape. Places sagging where they did not sag before. Wrinkles appearing before their time. A few pounds overweight that just will not go away. Are you ready for a 21-day miracle?

Can you think yourself thin? Can you think yourself rich? If that were possible, we would all have svelte bodies and a million dollars in our pockets.

Within three weeks, though, you will be well on your way to enjoying a slimmer you.

First of all, you do not want to "lose" weight. If you have lost something, you are looking to find it again. Do you really want those pounds to come back?

The first item on your list of things to observe is your relationship with food. Is it friend or foe? What are your limiting beliefs? Be aware of the times you eat and why. Do you use food for comfort? Why do you need to be comforted? What are the triggers? What do you eat? Do you exercise?

Much to think about that first week. Limiting beliefs, relationships, triggers, keeping track of what you eat.

Now that you know why reducing your weight is a challenge, you have the tools at hand to tackle that challenge. In week two, you reframe your thinking. You challenge those misbeliefs whenever they arise. You realize you, the person, are in control, not the food, not the body or the cravings. You begin to feel your power awakening.

Week three, make a plan. Buy the right foods, get the right amount of exercise, take nutrition classes, find new recipes. Do what you must do to meet your goal.

Week four and beyond. Congratulations! You are on your way to a sleeker you. Repeat this process whenever you feel bogged down. The second and third times around you will find other answers, have deeper insights. Have greater success.

Do you see how it works? From stuck to success in 21 days.

Stuck before because you did not know how to get out of your rut. Success now because you have discovered your potential and realize you are stronger than you believed.

In a way, this is "thinking yourself thin." But for "thinking" to become more than an idea, an action must follow the thought.

Thought + Action = Results

Chapter 5

THE IMPOSTER SYNDROME

The imposter syndrome is a result of being full of self-doubt. Authors go through this; not sure their work will be accepted. "Who do I think I am - an expert at anything, let alone this topic I am writing about. No one has read my other work, why should they read this?"

Does that sound familiar? This flood of self-doubt does not just occur with authors. Anyone can be hit with a blank page – stuck in your tracks.

Have you ever run into a brick wall? No matter what you try, you cannot seem to get under it or around it. And it is too high to climb.

The mind is a beautiful thing, but some days … not so much. Those are the days you second guess everything, the days that make you want to tear it all up and walk away. Why put in the effort?

Steven King felt the same way when he wrote *Carrie*. He threw it in the trash. His wife dug it out and told him to finish it.

You need a partner to egg you on, someone who believes in you when you do not. This is a prerequisite for a successful relationship. Total and unquestioning support. What if she had said, "You are so right, honey, you are not a writer! I'm glad you finally realized that." Where would the world be without Steven King and his stories?

Even the best feel like imposters at times, so do not beat yourself up because you feel like one, too. The only way to get rid of a blank page is to write on it. Once the writing starts, the frozen mind kicks into gear and the next thing you know, an entire page is filled up!

Brick by Brick. Make it stick. That is why every day, rain or shine, whether you feel like it or not, you must pursue your goal.

Writing is only an example. Whatever you do in life, if you want to succeed, you must talk yourself out of self-doubt.

Doubt is a sign of double-standards and instability.

How can you have faith if you doubt? Believing in yourself is having faith in yourself, and if you are full of doubt of your potential – well – need I say more?

It is a common mantra these days: Have positive thoughts and you will have a positive day. The opposite is true. Have negative thoughts and have a negative day.

Unfortunately, the human spirit is not static. It is always in a constant state of flux. Highs and lows from one minute to the next. Our bodies are a natural creation. Consider how nature can quickly change. One minute the sun is shining and the next minute – you never know. There could be a hurricane or a blizzard, depending on where you live. What do you do? You weather out the storm.

Learn to weather the storms of your emotions. Know that your day is in flux with highs and lows. It is natural for your moods to change throughout the day. That does not make you mentally "unstable." That makes you human. What a concept!

What makes you unstable are your doubts about your abilities. You cannot center on your goodness if you are criticizing who you are. Are you beset with anxiety? Your self-doubt may be the cause. Americans are anxious; anti-anxiety drugs are one of the most sought-after prescription drugs. Illegal drugs are at an all-time high. People turn to alcohol for a buzz and to relax.

These are the ways we cope with our overly anxious world. These are not good habits to get into, but sometimes you reach a point where you need more than self-control.

What you need more than anything is a strong dose of confidence! That is what your 21-day miracle will give you. You made it through 21 days, even though you wanted to quit. You did not quit.

There are many suggestions on how to deal with anxiety. If you suffered past trauma, safety is always an issue. Checking your environment to detect a threat, even when perfectly safe, is hard on the survival mechanism. What causes your anxiety? How do you handle it?

Getting over the imposter syndrome is a great topic for a 21-day miracle. Week one, observe. Answer the questions of how, why, and what. Week two, reframe. Catch your self-doubt in action and replace it. Find a word or phrase that you can use when these thinking patterns arise. "Stop!" "Think of something else!"

Retraining your brain is like training your pup to sit, stand, and lay down. What do you do with your pup? You give him a command. "Sit." You give him a treat. You pat him on the head and say, "Good boy." After a few times of that, he is happy to oblige. The same with your brain.

You are the captain of your fate, so be the captain.

Control your thoughts instead of them controlling you. Give your brain a command. "Stop." Reward yourself and say, "Good job!" We are pleasure seekers. We love to have our ears scratched, to be told we are doing good, to get a hug for a job well done.

Our partners often give us what we need, like Steven King's wife. Most of the time though, we are on our own. Left to scratch our own ears, to give ourselves that longed-for hug.

The next time you have anxiety, or feel a panic attack coming on, try this 5-minute trick.

Perform each task for one minute for a total of five minutes.

1. Clean a room.
2. Stand outside.
3. Interact with a living being – petting your pup is great for this.
4. Do a job on your to-do list.
5. Treat yourself to a self-soothing activity.

When the nervous system and the hormonal system are in balance, it takes 90 seconds for the chemical reactions of an emotion to leave your body. That is, if you let the moment pass and think nothing more of it.

These reactions stay, however, for as long as you think about the event. Perseverating. Running the scene over and over, cycling through mind and body until you decide to say, "STOP."

This 5-minute exercise is a great trick to distract your mind. After a while, like training your dog to sit, your brain will quickly become distracted. You will be able to chase those nasty thoughts away more quickly. In my book - that is a miracle in itself.

Week three: Make a plan. You discovered tools along the way to quell your self-doubt and imposter syndrome. Plan on how you will keep those tools handy so you can use them to staunch the flood of emotions before they get out of hand.

If you are plagued with self-doubt, feel that you are not worthy of accomplishing your goals, feel like an imposter, try the 21-day miracle. Get rid of that self-doubt and discover the creative and productive person inside of you. Tell procrastination to take a back seat.

Do not worry about tomorrow,
For tomorrow will worry about itself.
Matthew 6:34

Chapter 6

AND ON THE SEVENTH DAY, HE RESTED

The well-known story in the Book of Genesis about God creating heaven and earth make a point to let us know he did this in six days, and on the seventh day he rested.

Rest on the Seventh Day is a tradition in all major religions. There is a day set aside for worship and fellowship. The importance that was placed on resting the in old times cannot be lost on us today.

Rest is connotated in many ways in our world. Music has rests. The silence is as necessary as the music playing. Imagine a song with no flow, no rhythm, no breaks. Like swimming under water, finally coming up gasping for air. Top executives carve resting time into their day. They take a nap or sit quietly and review their day. It is this time away from the bustle of the business that helps a CEO do an upstanding job.

What does resting have to do with the 21-day miracle? Quite a bit.

It is okay to take a break.

Writers take breaks from writing; musicians take breaks from playing. Rather, they take breaks from the physical aspect, but their minds are at work, composing that song, writing that novel. It is a different kind of creativity; the physical part of writing is spewing out what you worked out in your head the days you *were not* writing. Composing a song, same thing. Visualization in action.

If an author or a composer can visualize a creation, why can't you?

If you want to be a millionaire, hang out with millionaires, even if you are not one. By osmosis and paying attention, one day you, too, will be a millionaire. First, though, you must be clear in your mind that you want to be wealthy and what you must do to obtain those riches.

What do you do? You dream. You think about all the wonderful piles of money you will be raking in, the high life, the financial security – the work that has to be done to get there. Oh, what a life! You dream about it all, you decide you want that life, and you figure out how to achieve it.

What are you doing? Visualizing your future. Seeing yourself with all those happy emotions being a happy, rich person.

This is how dreams come true. "I do dream about being rich, and I still am poorer than a church mouse," you say.

This is where rest, time, and patience come into play. Patience builds character. Character grows over time. Patience is a discipline that most of us are not good at. In our throw-away society, we want things NOW. Pay as you go in debt so you can fulfill your urge to have it NOW!

Even five minutes in a calm state is effective in lowering the stress hormones accumulated throughout the day. The goal is to relax and rest your mind. When thoughts intrude, let them pass through like clouds in the sky. Stay focused on breathing and calmness. Resting your nervous system. Over time, you will look forward to going into this relaxed state and your body and brain will respond more quickly to becoming calm.

What does resting have to do with your 21-day miracle? I must disqualify an earlier statement just a bit – I said to work on your goal 15 minutes a day every day. There are days when that 15-minute commitment just does not happen. Life gets in the way, and as you drift off to sleep you remember, you forgot to put in your 15 minutes. Or, if you are seriously stuck, it is hard to get off the couch for 15 minutes.

And that is the point of this exercise. Say your goal is to get off the couch and find something constructive to do. Just devote 15 minutes a day for three weeks, following the formula of Observe, Reframe, and Plan.

There are days when getting off the couch, except making it to the kitchen and a bathroom break, is a chore. When a bad day comes along, you cannot handle meeting your goal. It is just too much work.

I am sorry you are this deep in the dumps. After the 21-day miracle, though, you will feel better. On week two you look at your observations from week one and find an area on which you can work. What limiting beliefs did you discover? Are you full of self-doubt? Do you have social anxiety? Do you have a medical condition that makes you feel this way? Week two will give you answers, especially if you journal your thoughts.

Writing down thoughts and ideas gives you clarity, plus you can go back and review what you wrote. You begin to see a picture, and as we have seen earlier, visualization is most important for success.

Week three, you are ready to make a plan. What will it take to get you off the couch? Do you need to see a doctor, or a counsellor? What steps can you take to make your life easier on yourself?

And then Celebrate! You made it through! Even though you had to take a few breaks, a few days off, you persevered, you met your goal. Now that you know why you cannot get off the couch, why you are stuck, you are on the road to success, which is living a more productive life. You went from stuck to success in 21 days. This may seem like a small success, but now you have a foundation to grow more successes! Brick by brick, remember?

Breaks. Silence. The void.

It is this void that is useful. Think of a vase. The emptiness inside holds the water. Houses have doors and windows, creating a void so we can walk from room to room and see outside. Think about it. How many things in your world would be dysfunctional if they were not empty?

Energy at rest. Learn to take advantage of this energy, and you will walk through your day with more vigor. Simply because you stopped burning the candle at both ends and wasting your energy on unimportant things.

Give yourself a break. Eliminate the stressors, the toxins, from your life. They are energy wasters. The sooner you get rid of them, the sooner you will rest.

To illustrate the importance of rest, here is an excerpt from a great book on Eastern philosophy, the _Tao of Pooh_ by Benjamin Hoff. This is what Pooh has to say about how Americans, from the Puritans forward, melded and molded our heritage of this great land we call America.

The Tao of Pooh

The Puritans worked themselves to death in the fields without getting much in return. The wiser inhabitants of the land, who had lived there for centuries, showed them ways to work in harmony with the earth's rhythm.

Now you plant; now you relax. Now you work with the soil; now you leave it alone.

The Puritans never understood the second half of this advice. They would work the soil and plant. But were too driven to relax and leave it alone. After two or three generations of pushing, pushing, pushing the once-fertile earth, and a couple more centuries depleting its energy further with synthetic stimulants, there are now apples tasting like cardboard, oranges tasting like tennis balls, and pears tasking like sweetened Styrofoam.

Our ancestors failed to appreciate the beauty of the endless forests and clear waters appearing before them on this fresh, green continent of the new world. Instead, they saw the paradise and the people who lived in harmony with it as alien and threatening; people to attack and conquer.

From the miserable Puritans came the restless pioneer, and from them, the restless cowboy, always riding off into the sunset, looking for anything better just down the trail.

From our dissatisfied ancestry came the busy man, who like our forefathers, has never really felt at home, at peace with this friendly land. Rigid, combative, and unfriendly, he is tight-fisted and too hard on himself, too hard on others, and too hard on a world heroically carrying on despite what man is doing to it.

Real progress involves growing and developing, which involves changing inside. The urge to grow and develop, present in all forms of life, becomes perverted in modern man's mind. There is the constant struggle to change everything and everyone, and to interfere with things he has no business interfering with, including practically every lifeform on earth.

Now after centuries of pushing and over-cultivation, not relaxing and letting the land sit idle, we are a people who are stretched to the limit. We are challenged with the call to leave our old ways of thinking behind and to develop new ways of living.

Resting is important for success. Now you plant. Now you relax.

Chapter 7

POSSIBILITY THINKING

As you are putting together your miracle, you will discover talents you never thought you had. You are learning to shift your mindset from "I can't" to "I can!" This is not any easy task, one that requires patience and gentleness on your part. Listen to your self-talk. How do you relate to you? Are you kind and encouraging, or are you constantly finding fault with what you do? What is that voice in your head saying to you?

Those voices are merely memories from the past. Every limiting belief is a product of conditioning. The only way to get rid of your misbeliefs is to confront them head on. It is not "you" you are criticizing, but those negative thoughts that keep popping up during the day and night. We develop beliefs in childhood and reinforce them as adults. "I am worthless." Carrying this around in your head does indeed make you feel worthless, and most likely unproductive.

There is another way to think, one that is not fraught with stress and trauma. You wonder how some people have it all, and here you are, struggling. Wouldn't you like a life without struggle? That must be true since you are this far into this book.

Limiting beliefs makes us believe it is impossible to accomplish anything we attempt. Lack of motivation is a manifestation of this. A self-fulfilling prophecy, so to speak. We get hung up in the impossibilities of our situation, front and center, ahead of the game, convinced this task is impossible.

Possibility thinking is just the opposite.

Impossible translates into *I'm possible*. *I am possible*. Anything I do is possible. No matter how daunting the task, it is not beyond me, because I live in a world of possibilities where nothing can go wrong.

Thinking in possibilities is a novel approach to getting things done.

To illustrate this, here is a true story of a man who believed nothing was impossible, as told by Dr. Robert Schuller in his book, *Discover your Possibilities*.

Jack had a bare patch of yard that was difficult to water and grow grass. A useless space. He decided to lay brick over the patch, but to do this he first had to dig the soil deep enough so the brick was level with the rest of the yard.

He set out one morning determined to get as much done as he could. This was a long strip; four-feet wide and one-hundred feet long.

He brought out his tools; his wheelbarrow, rake, and shovel; and started to dig. He filled two or three wheelbarrows with dirt, took the dirt into his backyard, and started a pile. The day was getting warm; he started to sweat. By midmorning he had only a little bit dug, and a long way to go.

His neighbor came out and watched for a while before he asked, "What are you doing, son?"

"Filling this useless strip in my yard with brick," said Jack.

"You have a long way to go," said the neighbor. "Do you really believe you will finish this big job? And what do you plan to do with all the dirt?"

"I'm taking it in the back and starting a pile."

"And what happens after the pile gets too high? What are you going to do then?" inquired the neighbor.

Jack scratched his head and said, "Possibility thinking."

The neighbor shook his head and went about his day.

A short time later, Jack's friend, Will, stopped by. He was driving a truck and pulling a trailer with a tractor on it. He only stopped by for a minute to chat. Will had no plans to help Jack dig his useless plot. As they got to talking, Jack asked Will where he was going with his truck and the tractor. "On my way to a job," said Will.

A brilliant thought popped into Jack's head. If Will would use his tractor to dig the strip, in exchange, he could take the dirt.

In short order, the job was finished, Will went on his way with his load of dirt, and Jack was happily planning how to lay the bricks when his neighbor came home for lunch.

Amazed, the neighbor asked, "How did you work so fast?"

"Possibility thinking," exclaimed Jack.

A formula for bringing possibility into your life.

1. **Expect cheerful conditions.** Expectations play a large role in a success story. By expecting cheerful conditions, cheerful things happen. Jack did not know how the job was going to get done, he just cheerfully went about his business, knowing it would be done.
2. **Look for agreeable companions.** Jack's agreeable companion was Will. The neighbor not so much. Jack could have listened to the neighbor and said, "You are right. This is crazy. It is hot out and I do not have the right tools." But he did not quit. He found the right tools without even looking for them!
3. **Show a sincere, wholehearted interest in those around you and they will respond in same**. People love to be loved. They love to be heard. By taking the time to listen to them and establish a bond, you gain a friend.
4. **Listen to the warnings of negativity.** Negativity brings depression and lack of motivation. It is easy to talk yourself out of a job – and just as easy to talk yourself into a job. If you see the job finished in your mind's eye before you start, you will be amazed how quickly time flies. You are done before you know it.
5. **Replace the negative mental picture with possibilities.** Chase those thoughts away by bringing yourself into the *Now*. Bring your mind to the present. Anxiety is caused from worrying about the past. Stop worrying and start thinking in possibilities.
6. **Your future is what you make it.** Brick by brick. One 21-day miracle at a time.

When you begin to doubt yourself and feel the eight of the Imposter Syndrome, pause – and let those doubts go.

Doubting makes you double-minded and unstable. Doubt is lack of believing. Instead, believe in possibilities! Incorporate possibility thinking into your 21-day miracle. You will be amazed at the results.

I AM Possible!!

Chapter 8

"GOING THROUGH" IS NOT THE SAME AS "STUCK IN"

Once you start paying attention, you notice miracles are all around you. Once you begin to notice the little things, the miracles that surround you, then you know you are on the right track to enlightenment.

Enlightenment. A word tossed carelessly around these days. We are moving into a time of spiritual connectedness where people are more introspective and less tolerant of injustice. As a result of that movement, we see words like "mindfulness," "meditation," "enlightenment."

Right living. That is what it all boils down to. Living your life in the right way. What is the right way? That is up to you. We have free will, all of us. Even bogged down in a prison cell, there is still free will to make the best of it.

Two men in prison bars.
One sees mud. The other sees stars.

The man who sees mud has a miserable existence. The one who sees stars keeps his eyes on maintaining a positive attitude. If you want to survive prison, the ultimate test of human mettle, you must have a good attitude.

When stuck in a rut, you cannot see the light at the end of the tunnel. You feel like you are in a morass of blackness and see no way out. If you are stuck on the couch and cannot find your way off, you are definitely stuck in a rut.

Too many people today are glued to their iPhones and Androids. It is common to see a fine young person with a lot of potential wasting away in front of the keyboard, playing games. This is stuck in a rut. A rut very difficult to remove yourself from.

Or, you may be busy all day long, longing for a chance to sit on the couch. Instead, you are busy with work and chores and life, but you still feel stuck.

The feeling of stuckedness knows no boundaries.

You can be a millionaire and have a lousy love life. And you can also be the poorest man on earth and live in abundance.

How does that work? That is the difference between "going through" a life's experience and being "stuck." Attitude is everything. On the days your attitude is not the greatest, it is difficult to see the stars. That is okay. It is a natural human element to have good days and bad days. Being stuck in what is holding you back produces more bad days than good.

Transform those negative feelings into positive ones. Here is a trick that might help.

1. **Recognize the feeling when it arises**. – Observe, be a witness to your emotions.
2. **Become one with the feeling.** Feel the rush, what is your body feeling? Tell yourself you are more than this emotion. "I am more than my fear. I do not need to be afraid."
3. **Calm the feeling.** Release it, let it go. Reduce the impending overwhelm by attending to it in the moment. Use the five-minute technique mentioned earlier to move your mind away from your anxious thoughts.
4. **Ask yourself, "Why am I suffering?"** Desire causes suffering. Desire is wanting what we do not have. A dose of gratitude will put your desires into perspective, and you will no longer suffer.

We were taught to seek satisfaction from the external. Our accomplishments are awarded with praise and celebration. We feed on that need for assurance.

As humans, we need praise and pats on the back. Having approval from others activates our pleasure centers – those feel-good hormones run high.

But what happens when those accolades are no longer? Who is going to pat you on the back for your silent accomplishments? We have conditioned our true self into believing that external approval is all there is.

Hence, self-doubt and lack of motivation. When the crowds stop cheering, what do you do now?

Extreme highs are followed by extreme lows. If you want consistency and calmness in your life, you must let go of the belief that praise and success come from outside sources.

Take control of your emotions. You are the master – not your emotions, not the past nor the future. Shift your locus of control away from the external world and center it on your individuality. When that happens, you know you are on the path to enlightenment.

After all, isn't that what this life is about? To 'go through" life's difficulties and not become "stuck" in the middle? To find fulfilling endeavors and relationships that bring us pleasure and not pain?

The Chinese have a term, *daomei*. There is not a translation for it, but the closest is negative thinking. It is a phrase they use to remind whoever is making the comment that their negative thinking will get them nowhere. Their philosophy is "if you think *daomei, daomei* will happen."

The only way out of a tunnel is to go through it. Use this 21-day miracle plan and watch your dreams stop being "stuck." Congratulations, you have entered the "going through" process of change.

Feeling stuck is DAOMEI

Chapter 9

AFTERTHOUGHTS

As we have seen, changing your life is not an overnight, life-shattering, event. True, changes can happen that way; one minute things are normal and the next they are not. Changes are hard to see. If you stick with your plan, over time you will begin to see the results of your efforts. That is progress.

You are full of possibilities. Are you ready to realize your potential? Now you know the formula to move forward.

Observe, Reframe and Plan, all in 21 days: your possibilities are limitless.

The secret is to immerse yourself in what you want to accomplish. Read, study, and learn everything you can that pertains to your goal. Knowledge is power. The more knowledge you acquire, the more you empower yourself to surge ahead. Immersion also propels you forward. Before you know it, the 21 days are over. Where did the time go?

The most important takeaway for success is to find your passion by knowing what you are best at. The economic engine will drive right into your driveway if you know these two things. Do what you love, and the money will follow. What do you love? Of all your talents, which one describes you the best, gives you the most passion?

Do not get the 21-day miracle mixed up with 21 days to break a habit. At the most, that theory is junk science, at the least, it depends on the person and the habit.

Here, we are not breaking habits. We are changing an aspect of our life.

A cluttered house reveals a cluttered mind.
When your house is in order, your mind is in order.
-Old Chinese Proverb-

Changing the cat box regularly is a "smelly" example of how improving on one simple chore can make all the difference in how your house smells and how you feel.

The whole point of this exercise is to put your mind in order, is it not? Whatever problem you chose to solve in 21 days, you are doing it for self-improvement, or why would you waste your time?

Why, indeed. A good question when met with the imposter syndrome. What is the point in what you are doing, you know you will fail anyway. Change that by thinking in possibilities. When Jack started digging his plot of land, you can be sure his mind was working on ways to make the job easier. Work smarter, not harder. By opening his mind to potential solutions, the seemingly impossible happened. If this worked for Jack, why can't it work for you? Possibility thinking.

The 21-day miracle is about accomplishing your goals, not necessarily abolishing bad habits. The bad habits will naturally disappear. Change is elusive. One day you realize you no longer crave the cigarette or another long session scrolling on your phone. You have found other ways, more constructive ways, to fill your time. If you are no longer stuck in a rut, that is a miracle in itself.

Go ahead. Try out a miracle. You will be amazed.

WHY THIS WORKS

Jack was not just thinking, he was also visualizing ways to make his job easier. We think in pictures, and when visualizing yourself as successful, your brain looks around for the physical picture. What seems like a coincidence; accidentally finding a book that relates to what you are thinking about, or seeing a video that you needed to hear; may not be coincidences at all, but our brain searching for answers and putting them in front of us.

Have you ever lost your true love and everywhere you look, all you see are couples holding hands? Success works the same way.

How amazing is it that you can learn to fly a multi-billion-dollar jet plane in three weeks? The Army is not trusting you to fly solo at that point, but still. There is no minimizing this accomplishment. But as I have shown throughout this book, it is not just fighter pilots that can learn to fly in 21 days.

Success comes in small increments. Most of the time you do not even see it. We expect big brass bands and tons of fanfare for our accomplishments. If you are like most of us, our fan base is slim to none. When it comes down to it, the only cheerleader is yourself. Or, you can have three of them. Me, myself, and I!

Breaking a problem into a three-part solution, as suggested throughout this book, allows small increments of success to become a celebration: To pat ourselves on the back, to tell ourselves it was a job well done. The end of the 21 days reminds us to reward our efforts.

Observe, Reframe and Plan lays a blueprint for easily solving a problem. Because there is a short timeline, the goal is visible. Three weeks? Quite doable.

By starting with something easy to fix, but will make a significant difference, self-limiting doubt is pushed back a step or two. Courage and pride enter and says, "Look what we did!" This offers a strong handle to grasp when confidence weakens.

The bonus is you are so happy with the results that you will look for other things in your life that could use a little miracle work.

You may have to revisit the same problem several times. Each time you do, you gain different insight because you study the problem from a changed perspective. The goal here is to gain confidence in your actions. To know that you have the ability to tackle any problem that comes along, no matter how taxing it is, and solve it.

This is not saying you will not go through angst. No decision in the making is worth it unless there's agony. That is part of the process. Angst and agony; especially that first week. Observing your thoughts and actions without judgement is a tough task. But then you get a chance to reframe your angst and agony into confidence and power,

These are just a few of the reasons why this plan for a 21-day miracle works. You will find your own.

Good luck. Peace be with you.

c.w. Pickett

c.w. Pickett grew up in an era when kindness and civility were the norm, and violence was something heard about in the news rather than experienced daily. Through her books, she encourages a return to that sense of goodness while addressing the causes and prevention of the growing violence in society.

Her writing is informed by twenty years of research, firsthand experience, and a lifelong commitment to helping others. She is the founder of Pickett's Reflections, LLC, a mission-driven endeavor focused on building families and touching lives.

Writing, for Pickett, is both a calling and a means of making sense of a world in chaos. Her personal seal, "Chaos," embodies this journey:

"Out of chaos, a star is born."

To learn more about her work, visit **www.cwpickett.com**.

www.ingramcontent.com/pod-product-compliance
Lightning Source LLC
Chambersburg PA
CBHW041624110426

42740CB00042BA/43